At the Animal Hospital

This book is dedicated to
the good people at
the Webster Groves Animal Hospital,
Webster Groves, Missouri.

Grateful acknowledgment is made to
John W. Hatfield, V.M.D.
Urban Veterinary Care
Chicago, Illinois

Design and Art Direction
Lindaanne Donohoe Design

Library of Congress Cataloging-in-Publication Data
Greene, Carol.
At the animal hospital/Carol Greene.
p.   cm.
Summary: Describes the various activities of veterinarians,
technicians, office workers, and cleaners at a veterinary hospital.
ISBN 1-56766-290-0 (lib. bdg.)
1. Veterinary hospitals—Juvenile literature.
[1. Veterinary hospitals. I. Title.
SF604.55.G74   1996   96-14015
636.08'32—DC20   CIP
                                                   AC

At the Animal Hospital

By Carol Greene

Photographs by Phil Martin

The Child's World®

The animal hospital looks small and quiet.
But five veterinarians work inside.
So do seven technicians, four office workers,
and a cleaner.

Animal hospitals
are busy places.

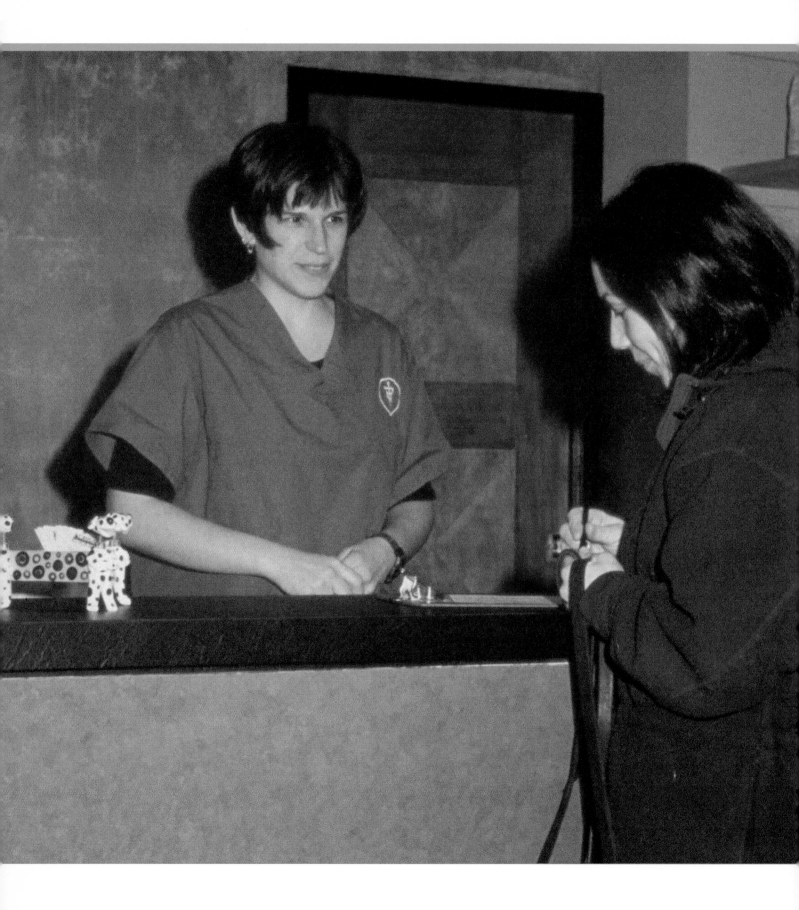

BRRING!

Click, click, click!

"Hello!"

An office worker is at the front desk.

She answers phones and welcomes people.

She also makes appointments and adds

up bills on the computer.

Sometimes she does all these things at once.

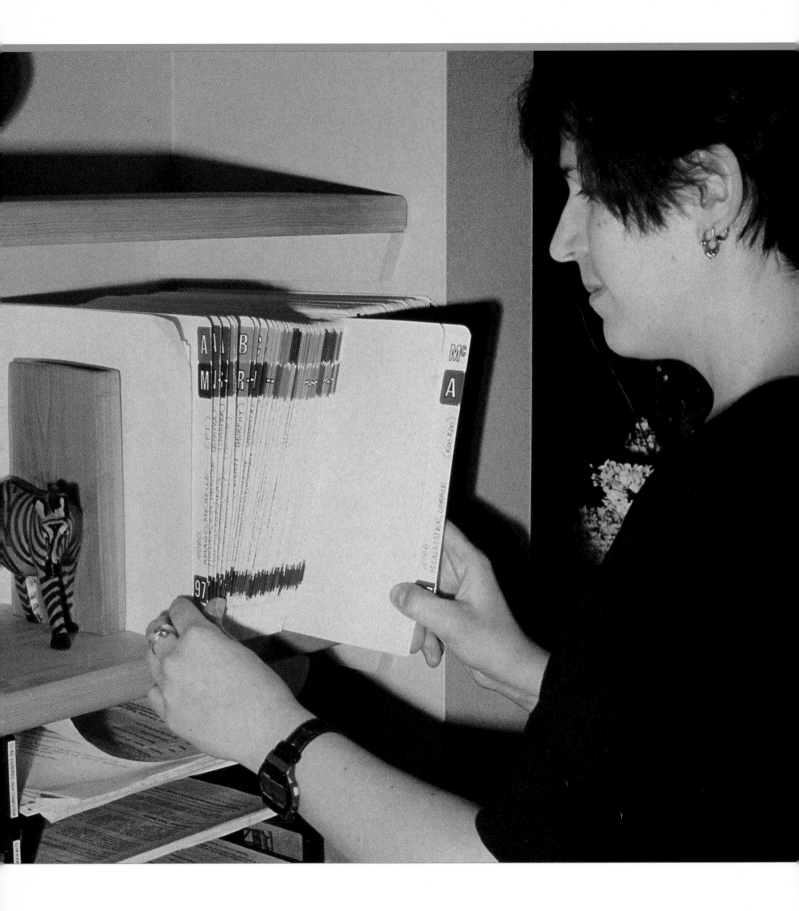

Important facts about each animal are kept in the computer. The information is written down and kept in folders too.

Office workers help the vet find the right folder.

Vets check out the animals in examination rooms. These rooms have high tables, sinks, and cabinets.

Of course you can't put a cow on a high table. Country vets see their patients on the farm or in the barn.

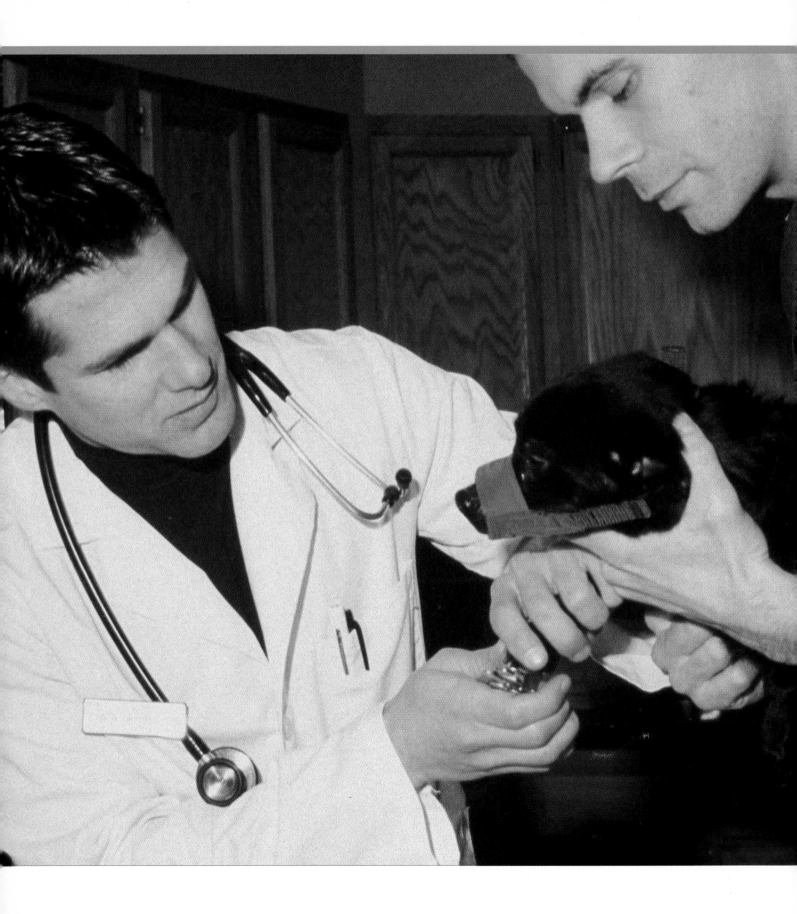

If an animal needs special treatment, the vet takes it to the treatment room. A helper often holds the animal while the vet works on it.

Sometimes vets put muzzles on dogs so they won't bite.

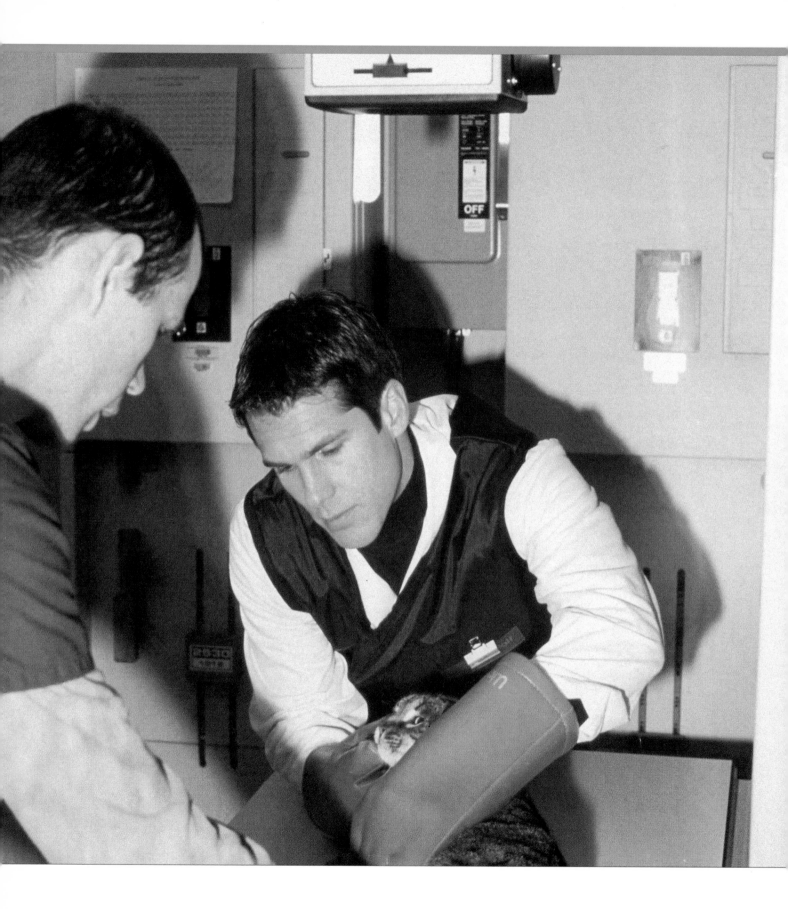

BZZZZ!

When an animal needs an X ray,

the vet uses the hospital's X-ray machine.

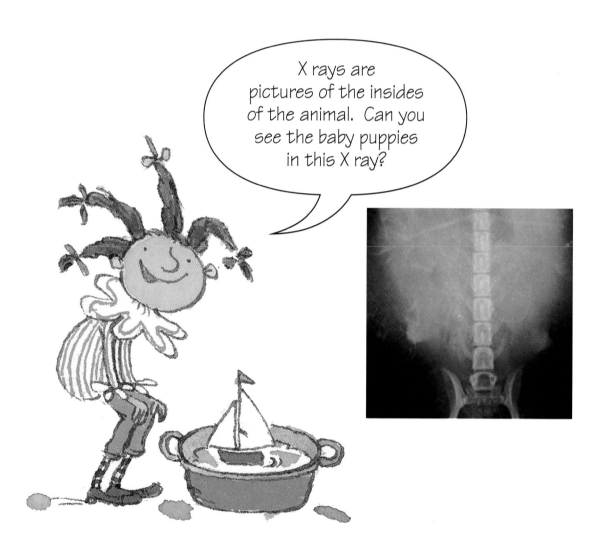

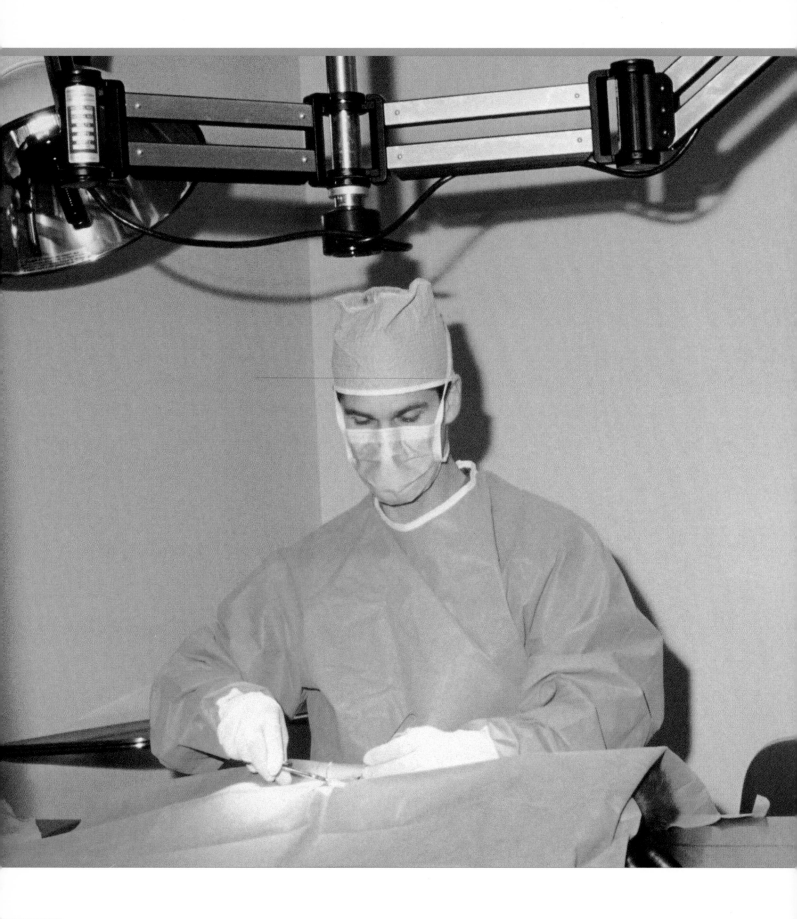

Vets perform operations on animals.

The hospital's operating room is bright and shiny.

The lab has many instruments that help vets.
The microscope makes tiny creatures
in the animal's body look much bigger.
Then the vet can tell what they are.

Some tiny creatures can make an animal sick.

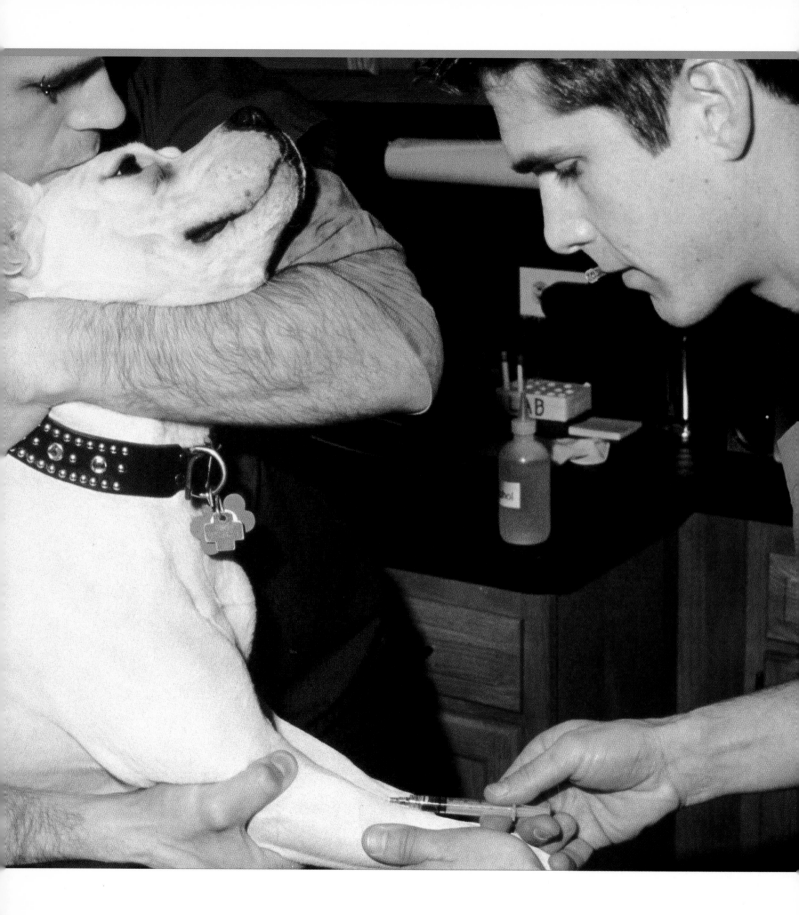

The vet takes a sample of this dog's blood. This helps the vet figure out what is wrong with him.

THUMP! THUMP! WHRRRR!

You probably have machines like
these at home—a washer and a dryer.
Animal hospitals need them too.

Animal hospitals
use piles of towels
and blankets
each day.

Sometimes sick animals have to be
at the animal hospital for a while.
They stay in cages.

WOOF! YIP! YIP! YIP! MEOW!
These animals are not sick at all.
They are boarders. Some owners
leave their pets at the animal hospital
when the owners go away.

Don't worry.
Your owners
will be back.

Cats have litter boxes in their cages.

But most dogs go to the bathroom outside.

The animal hospital has a special place for that too.

Sometimes there are messes anyway.

Everyone helps clean up.

But cleaners do the really good cleaning.

Cleaners often work at night when the animal hospital is quiet.

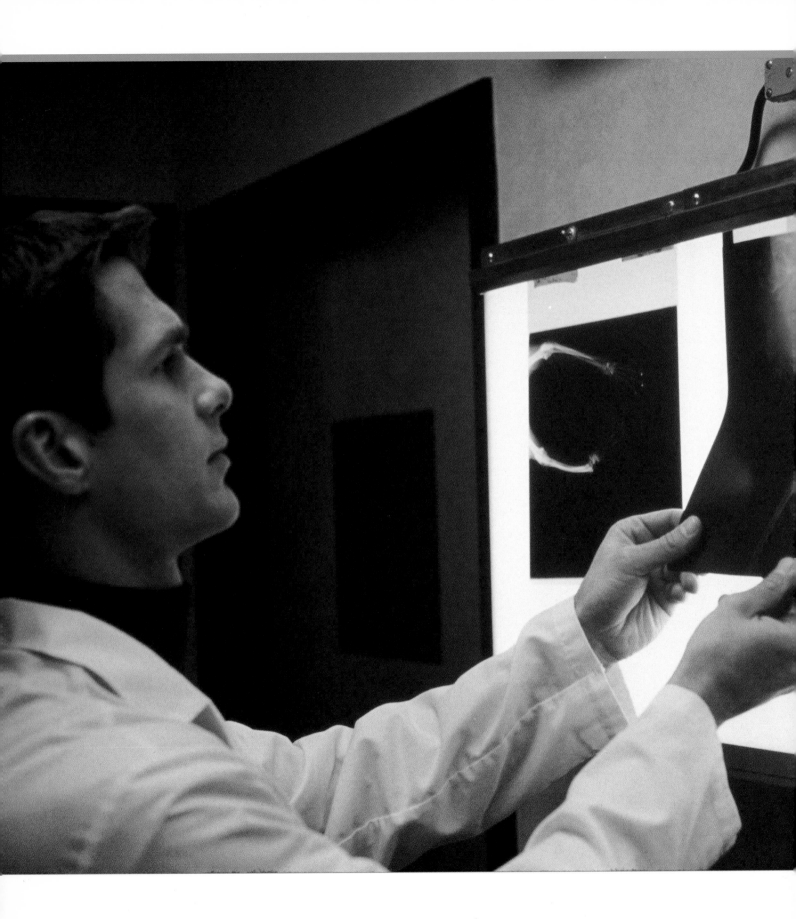

Veterinarians need offices.

Sometimes several vets share one office.

There they can read X rays, make phone calls, or just think.

Yoo Hoo!
Your next patient
is here!

Glossary

microscope (MY kruh skohp)   a device that allows people to see very small things

muzzle (MUHZ uhl)   a covering for an animal's mouth

veterinarian (veh truh NER ee uhn)   a doctor who takes care of animals

About the Author

Carol Greene has written over 200 books for children. She also likes to read books, make teddy bears, work in her garden, and sing. Ms. Greene lives in Webster Grover, Missouri.